$12.95

D0166665

THE PRACTICAL STRATEGIES SERIES
IN GIFTED EDUCATION

series editors
FRANCES A. KARNES & KRISTEN R. STEPHENS

Teaching Culturally Diverse Gifted Students

Donna Y. Ford & H. Richard Milner

PRUFROCK PRESS, INC.

Printed in the United States of America.
ISBN-13: 978-1-59363-176-5
ISBN-10: 1-59363-176-6

At the time of this book's publication, all facts and figures cited are the most current available. All telephone numbers, addresses, and Web site URLs are accurate and active. All publications, organizations, Web sites, and other resources exist as described in the book, and all have been verified. The authors and Prufrock Press, Inc., make no warranty or guarantee concerning the information and materials given out by organizations or content found at Web sites, and we are not responsible for any changes that occur after this book's publication. If you find an error, please contact Prufrock Press, Inc. We strongly recommend to parents, teachers, and other adults that you monitor children's use of the Internet.

Prufrock Press, Inc.
P.O. Box 8813
Waco, Texas 76714-8813
(800) 998-2208
Fax (800) 240-0333
http://www.prufrock.com

Contents

The Practical Strategies Series in Gifted Education offers teachers, counselors, administrators, parents, and other interested parties up-to-date instructional techniques and information on a variety of issues pertinent to the field of gifted education. Each guide addresses a focused topic and is written by scholars with authority on the issue. Several guides have been published. Among the titles are:

- *Acceleration Strategies for Teaching Gifted Learners*
- *Curriculum Compacting: An Easy Start to Differentiating for High-Potential Students*
- *Enrichment Opportunities for Gifted Learners*
- *Independent Study for Gifted Learners*
- *Motivating Gifted Students*
- *Questioning Strategies for Teaching the Gifted*
- *Social & Emotional Teaching Strategies*
- *Using Media & Technology With Gifted Learners*

For a current listing of available guides within the series, please contact Prufrock Press at (800) 998-2208 or visit http://www.prufrock.com.

The 21st century is witnessing an unprecedented change in its demographics, especially in school settings. Like no other time in history, our nation is becoming overwhelmingly diverse, with Hispanic Americans and African Americans increasing in numbers. However, as our nation and schools become more diverse, we have witnessed little demographic changes relative to diversity in gifted education classes, programs, and services. That is to say, culturally and linguistically diverse students (Black, Hispanic, and Native American) are underrepresented in gifted education programs. Further, where diversity is concerned, there is the opposite demographic trend among the teaching profession, which has remained extensively White. These changes—reverse trends and demographics—carry important implications for the field of gifted education relative to changes that may need to be made in policy and practice.

Unfortunately, gifted education has not been proactive or aggressive at responding to issues of underrepresentation and addressing the needs of students from ethnically and culturally diverse backgrounds. Noticeably absent in the discussion of services, programming, and instruction, including differentiation, has been attention to issues of diversity (Ford, 1998, 2002). A review of the gifted education literature on topics ranging from identification to programming points to a picture of homogeneity and lack of differentiation in actual practice. Homogeneity is most blatant in areas of identification, definitions, instruction, and curriculum (Ford, Grantham, & Harris, 1998; Ford & Harris, 1999; Frasier, Garcia, & Passow, 1995; Frasier & Passow, 1994; Passow & Frasier, 1996). For example, even with increasing diversity in the United States, gifted programs tend to be extensively White and middle class. Despite the reality that students of color tend not to perform well on traditional tests, most schools rely extensively on testing alone to identity students as gifted (Colangelo & Davis, 2003; Davis & Colangelo, 2004; Ford, 2004). Regardless of efforts to reverse this pattern, most schools define giftedness in terms of cutoff scores and standard deviations. Despite newer and more contemporary definitions and theories of intelligence and giftedness, most schools only recognize and serve two types of giftedness—the academically gifted and intellectually gifted; less often do schools identify and serve gifted students in the visual and performing arts, leadership, and creativity. And despite the call for increased integration of multicultural content in the curriculum, curriculum for gifted students seldom has a multicultural focus (Ford & Harris, 1999).

The history of gifted education, compared to special education, is a short one, and the history of addressing the needs of gifted students who are culturally diverse is even briefer. In reading the literature in gifted education, it is apparent that several topics dominate the discussion: (1) how to define giftedness; (2) how to identify gifted students; and (3) how to serve gifted students (e.g., acceleration versus enrichment, etc.). Regardless of the content of the publications, a major theme is that, for gifted students to reach their potential, they must be appropriately identified, assessed, and served. We have aggressively promoted the belief that gifted students can only reach their full potential and capacity in school settings if they are given an education that meets their particular needs (Colangelo & Davis, 2003; Davis & Rimm, 2004; Ford & Harris, 1999; VanTassel-Baska, 1994). Too often, teachers have taught gifted students by offering more of the same level of material; providing either enrichment or acceleration alone; focusing only on cognitive growth in isolation from affective, physical, or intuitive growth; teaching high-level thinking skills in isolation from academic content; presenting additional work that is slightly different from the core curriculum; and/or grouping students with intellectual peers without differentiating content and instruction (National Association for Gifted Children, 1994).

Recognizing that gifted education must be more than quantitatively different from general education—not just more of the same—scholars have developed various curricular and instructional models to serve gifted students. While there are differences in these models, all of them support the philosophy that differentiated services must be provided for gifted students, specifically modifying the pace, depth, and breadth of curriculum and instruction relative to content, process, environment, and products. At minimal, differentiation, according to the National Association for Gifted Children (1994) includes: (1) acceleration of content; (2) in-depth study; (3) a high degree of complexity; (4) advanced content; and/or (5) variety in content and form. Some examples of delivery models that address at least one of these areas of differentiation include acceleration, enrichment, high-level thinking skills, flexible grouping, and compacting.

These strategies to differentiate curricula and instruction for gifted students address modifications in at least four major areas: content, process, product, and learning environment (see Maker & Nielson, 1995; Tomlinson, 1995, 1999; VanTassel-Baska, 1994). Strategies for content differentiation include presenting content that is related to broad-based issues, problems, and themes; multidisciplinary approaches to teaching; streamlining content; and organizing content to emphasize high-level skills and concepts. Strategies for process differentiation include an emphasis on independent or self-directed study; a focus on open-ended tasks; and in-depth learning on selected topics, particularly those of interest to the gifted student (Karnes & Bean, 2004). In terms of products, differentiation provides students with opportunities to apply and synthesize what they have learned. Sample strategies include the development of products that focus on real-world problems, the creation of products that challenge existing ideas and produce new ones, and other products beyond paper-and-pencil tasks (e.g., writing papers, taking test, etc.; Karnes & Stephens, 1999). Finally, differentiating the learning environment includes a focus on self-understanding, self-efficacy, and self-direction, in addition to helping students develop a positive and proactive attitude toward learning. All of these strategies are utilized with gifted students at the center of the teaching and learning process.

In the following pages, we build upon the existing body of work on gifted students by describing promising practices for working with students who are not only gifted, but also culturally diverse. Our model or framework is a simple one, and can be described using a Venn diagram (see Figure 1). In meeting the needs of culturally diverse gifted students, it is essential that we do so by considering their different needs as students who are gifted *and* as students who are culturally diverse. A common statement in gifted education is that gifted students are gifted 24 hours a day, seven days of the week (Ford & Harris, 1999). Likewise, culturally diverse students are culturally diverse 24 hours a day, 7 days of the week. Thus, we contend that the most effective way to teach and reach gifted students is to consider the combined needs associated with being gifted on one hand and being diverse on the other. The strategies described herein represent an amalgamation from two fields of education: gifted education and urban or multicultural education. In effect, two fields are bridged to meet the dual needs of the students under discussion.

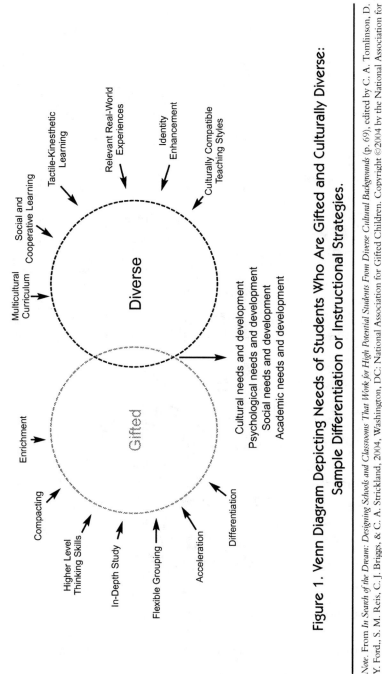

Figure 1. Venn Diagram Depicting Needs of Students Who Are Gifted and Culturally Diverse: Sample Differentiation or Instructional Strategies.

Note. From *In Search of the Dream: Designing Schools and Classrooms That Work for High Potential Students From Diverse Cultural Backgrounds* (p. 69), edited by C. A. Tomlinson, D. Y. Ford., S. M. Reis, C. J. Briggs, & C. A. Strickland, 2004, Washington, DC: National Association for Gifted Children. Copyright ©2004 by the National Association for Gifted Children.

Effective Teaching Strategies:
Sample Philosophical Orientations

Before delving further, an overview of philosophies that hold much promise for guiding the work of teachers is necessary. In this section, we focus on 11 perspectives of teaching and learning that have shown to be influential when working with students.

Prior to teaching, it is important—even necessary—that educators explore, develop, and then adopt an overarching philosophy of teaching and learning. This need seems especially important when teachers work with students who are culturally different from themselves. As a wealth of literature contends, gifted students have needs that differ from those of general education students; likewise, culturally diverse students have needs that differ from other students. Clearly, then, developing teaching strategies that help students reach their capacity is critical during these times of reform and as we consider the complexities inherent in the various needs students bring to classrooms and school settings.

To be effective with their students, teachers must develop a repertoire of knowledge, skills, beliefs, and values that allow them to teach well—strategies that allow teachers to teach in any context with various groups of students and with a range of student needs, interests, and skills in mind. The teaching strategies outlined in this section are shared as one way to place forthcoming ideas, recommendations, and strategies into perspective. All are framed by assumptions regarding how students learn or come to understand what is being taught.

Self-Reflective Instruction

Teachers' self-perception and introspection are central for helping students to succeed academically. An important dimension of this philosophy is that of "knowing thyself." Self-reflective teachers are better positioned to observe, understand, and develop tentative hypotheses about the academic and instructional needs of their students. Minimally, teachers should: (a) be familiar with their own learning and teaching styles; (b) be familiar with their strengths and shortcomings as an instructor, including, for example, subject matter knowledge, and an understanding about student learning and development; and (c) be familiar with their biases, stereotypes, and likes and dislikes about working with gifted students and culturally diverse students.

Inquiry-Based Instruction

Teachers should develop researcher lenses in their practice in order to meet the needs of students. Thus, action research and other research-based instruction are important. The teacher has to be willing to decide that he or she is not the only, or the most significant, arbiter of knowledge. Because students also bring a wealth of knowledge and experience to the classroom and learning environment, teachers need to be inquisitive about both their own needs and students' needs and experiences in order to take them into consideration when designing lessons. In short, teachers must find out what they as teachers know and what students know, how they came to know, and use this information to adjust their instruction. Teachers who are unwilling to be self-reflective run the risk of improperly teaching their students and otherwise contributing to students' disinterest in and disengagement from the learning process.

Blended Direct and Student Centered Instruction

When teachers understand that there are areas of expertise that their students bring into the learning environment, they simultaneously come to understand that they themselves bring something into the learning context as well. There may be times when instruction should follow a more direct orientation, where the teacher lectures and writes on the chalkboard or overhead. While some researchers, theoreticians, and practitioners would frown upon such an approach, we are suggesting that, in some instances, this approach is needed and thus necessary in order to have a truly shared knowledge approach to instruction, where both teachers and students are teaching and learning. Direct instruction may be more critical, for example, when teachers are introducing new or unfamiliar content. However, even when instruction is direct, it is necessary to connect it to the student. The examples used, the activities selected, and the discussions held, should be consistent with who the students are and what they bring into the classroom.

Meeting the Needs of the Whole Child

Teachers are often prepared to focus on the academic and cognitive needs of students, and rightfully so. But teaching "from the neck up" ignores the feelings and emotions—*the heart*—of students. Teachers must not only address the cognitive and academic needs of their students, they must also endeavor to meet students' affective, social, emotional, and cultural needs. The idea is that, when such needs are met, students' academic engagement improves.

Critical Thinking and Problem Solving

Much has been written about promoting critical thinking and problem solving among students in order to increase their achievement and test performance. Students who are encouraged to ask questions, to pose problems, to critique, and to interrogate what is presented to them are in a better position to truly use and to apply what they have been taught. For instance, with Bloom's Taxonomy (1956), Richard Paul's work (Paul & Elder, 2002), and Future Problem Solving as models, teachers are positioned to teach children not just what to think, but *how* to think. Accordingly, students are able to transfer knowledge from one academic task to another, and build and expand their knowledge because they understand how to think.

Real-Life Learning Experiences

Teachers who are effective at bringing learning to life—real life as experienced by their students—are often successful at promoting not only their students' learning, but also their students' interest in learning. Such teachers are able to make a personal connection between pedagogy and the lives of their students. The examples teachers use to make a point, to move students' thinking to higher levels, or to elicit student input are very important to students' engagement and ultimate success. To illuminate, students expect and deserve to know how what they are learning is relevant to their immediate and future lives and experiences. To be effective at focusing on real-life experiences, teachers must get to know their students; they must keep abreast of the multiple interests and talents of their students, so they might develop a good idea of the students' learning, experiences, and career trajectories.

Expertise Among All Students

Although this publication focuses on gifted students, teachers must assume that all students have strengths and some level of expertise. In this sense, teachers must realize that students may be highly creative, innovative, and have cutting edge ideas that are inconsistent with the teachers' experiences and ways of thinking. Teachers must, therefore, be willing to allow students to realize and reach their capacity by providing space for students to explore and to express this expertise; thus, teachers must recognize the myriad of strengths that students bring into the learning environment and encourage this knowledge development and expansion by providing pedagogical strategies that allow students to share and to expand their expertise.

Multicultural Knowledge and Competence

This philosophical position suggests that there is a serious need for teachers to have a solid foundation and knowledge base in terms of working with culturally diverse students. Our school districts are more diverse than ever before and teachers who choose to ignore issues of diversity set themselves—and their students—up for failure in many ways. That is to say, teachers can no longer afford to adopt "colorblind," "culture-blind," and "diversity-blind" ideologies in their teaching (Ford et al., 2003). Teachers must recognize the historical and contemporary issues that frame the experiences of culturally diverse students, and use those unique experiences to make connections, to bridge issues, and to create effective pedagogy. Teachers must seek to become culturally sensitive, culturally aware, culturally knowledgeable and, ultimately, culturally competent. Teachers should realize—and believe—that while they may be culturally and racially different from their students, they can still develop culturally relevant and specific instructional strategies.

Develop Teacher-Student Relationships

Teaching is more than instructing; it is also building relationships with students. Effective teachers are familiar with the maxim, "Students don't care what you know until they know that you care." With this belief serving as one foundation of their work, teachers attempt diligently to be more than outsiders with respect to their students and the communities in which they teach. Some teachers may commute from outside of the community where they teach. In order to develop substantive relationships with students and their communities, these teachers must attend social gatherings (whether it be a church function, a community cookout, a play, or a baseball game), visit the homes of their students, and even do some grocery shopping in the community in order to establish visibility, caring, and commitment. Ultimately, this reaching out and becoming immersed in the community creates strong teacher-student relationships. When teachers participate in their students' communities outside of the school day, they are able to make connections with their students because they see a world beyond the regular school day that can be incorporated into the lessons.

Range of Instructional Skills and Strategies

To date, no single instructional style can be advocated for meeting the needs of all students. Therefore, teachers, like all professionals, must have a range of tools to use when working with students. Teachers who have a limited, homogeneous set of teaching skills and strategies do a disservice to their students. For the sake of their students, teachers should learn to modify their teaching/instructional styles so that all students have access to the curriculum, and subsequently, an opportunity to learn.

In addition to the above philosophical orientations that should be held by all teachers, we offer another set of suggestions tied specifically to instruction. The next section presents an overview of recommended strategies often suggested in gifted education.

Gifted Education:
Recommended Instructional Strategies

Compared to students in general, gifted students have unique needs associated with both being gifted and with being *different* from other students. For example, relative to cognition, these students tend to be abstract thinkers; curious or inquisitive; insightful; and independent thinkers. Gifted students often see connections and relationships that others do not see and have an extensive vocabulary, often enjoying experimentations and the manipulation of ideas (Colangelo & Davis, 2003; Davis & Rimm, 2004).

Gifted students are also more likely than other students to have a gap in noncognitive areas of development, referred to as *asynchrony* (e.g., NAGC, 1995; Silverman, 1993). While they may be mentally and academically advanced, gifted students may lag behind in social and emotional maturity. In terms of social and affective development, gifted students may have more challenges than other students in finding true peers, an agemate who they can identify with intellectually and socially. This concept of *dyssynchrony* can take its toll on gifted students who have trouble finding someone to relate to beyond their intellectual and academic interests (Silverman, 1993). Educators—teachers, administrators, counselors, and psychologists—who are not familiar with, ignore, or minimize the various needs of gifted students are likely to be ineffective with them.

This last argument, formulated differently, also holds true for culturally diverse students; educators who are not familiar with, who ignore, or who minimize the various needs of diverse students are likely to be ineffective with them (Ford et al., 2000, 2002; Ford & Harris, 1999). In essence, we must ask ourselves, how are we responding to student differences? What are the effects of ignoring the needs of students who are gifted? What are the effects of ignoring the needs of students who are culturally diverse? What are the effects of ignoring the needs of students who are gifted *and* culturally diverse? Stated another way, how can we address the needs of students who are gifted? How can we address the needs of students who are culturally diverse? How can we address the needs of students who are gifted *and* culturally diverse?

Americans have a love-hate relationship with gifted students whereby the products of talent are valued, but services to gifted students are viewed as elitist and anti-democratic. The initial, sporadic, and short-lived emphasis on gifted education raised many of the problems advocates of gifted education face today: under-funding, under-staffing, and a general inattentiveness to the needs of gifted students. As Zirkel and Stevens (1987) reported, of the estimated 2.5 to 3.0 million gifted children[1] in the nation, only 1.2 million participate in special programs for gifted students. Consequently, even those districts providing gifted education often fail to serve all of their qualifying students.

Gifted education is not federally mandated; so, states do not have to identify or provide gifted education services. Thus, like

---

1. This figure is based on students who score in the top 3–5% on intelligence tests. It, therefore, underestimates the number of gifted students in general, as well as those not served. If one adopts a talent pool perspective, the number of gifted students would be greater. The figure also ignores gifted students with strengths in creativity, visual and performing arts, leadership, and academics.

students of color, gifted students frequently face educational neglect. The National Commission on Excellence (1983) stated, "most gifted students should be provided with a curriculum enriched and accelerated beyond the needs of other students of high ability" (p. 8). Gifted students require a more intensive and individualized curriculum, more challenging tasks, increased opportunities for creative expression and enrichment, in addition to practical guidance and experience. More recently, Davis and Rimm (2004) identified several goals of gifted education:

1. to provide programs to help meet the psychological, social, educational, and vocational needs of gifted students;

2. to help students become more capable of intelligent choice, independent learning, problem solving, and self-initiated action;

3. to strengthen skills and abilities in problem solving, creative thinking, communication, independent study, and research;

4. to reinforce individual interests;

5. to bring capable and motivated students together for support and intellectual stimulation;

6. to maximize learning and individual development, while minimizing boredom, confusion, and frustration; and

7. to help gifted students realize their potential and their contributions to self and society (p. xv).

Following are ways to meet these goals, focusing extensively on the concept of differentiation.

Differentiation: Teaching Gifted Students

Regardless of the model of delivery a school adopts to serve its gifted students, the concept of differentiation lays the foundation for gifted education curriculum. Effective curriculum and instruction for gifted students modifies content, process, product, and learning environment.

An effective curriculum for gifted students is first and foremost the general education curriculum, which is modified to meet their needs. The unique characteristics of the students serve as the basis for decisions on how the curriculum should be modified. Gifted education programs and services that build upon the characteristics and needs of gifted students are *qualitatively* different from the general education curriculum; a differentiated curriculum for gifted students is not based on quantitative adaptations (e.g., more work).

Modifying Process. To modify process, teachers must redesign or restructure activities to be more intellectually demanding. For example, students need to be challenged by questions that require a higher level of response or by open-ended questions that stimulate inquiry, active exploration, and discovery. The goal is for students to think about subjects in more abstract, multi-layered, and complex ways.

Modifying Content. Content can be modified through acceleration, compacting, variety, reorganization, flexible pacing, and the use of more advanced or complex concepts, abstractions, and materials. Content consists of ideas, concepts, descriptive information, and facts (Berger, 1991).

Modifying Products. Teachers can encourage students to demonstrate what they have learned in various ways that reflect both knowledge and ability (Berger, 1991). Ideally, products should address real problems, concerns, and audiences (Karnes & Stephens, 1999).

Modifying Environment. All students learn best in democratic, nonjudgmental, student-centered environments; however, gifted students appear to require more independence and opportunities to explore and inquire in a nonthreatening setting.

Characteristics of a Differentiated Class

According to Tomlinson (1995, 1999), at least three characteristics shape teaching and learning in an effective differentiated classroom:

1. Instruction is concept focused and principle driven. Gifted students are given the opportunity to explore and apply the key concepts and principles of subjects being studied. This type of instruction helps student to grasp and use powerful ideas and encourages them to expand their understanding and application of the key concepts and principles. Such instruction stresses understanding or conceptualization rather than retention and regurgitation of fragmented bits of information (Berger, 1991).

2. Flexible grouping is used. In a differentiated class, students work in many grouping arrangements. Students may work alone, in pairs, and in groups. Arrangements can be made based on readiness, interests, and/or learning styles. In a differentiated classroom, whole-group instruction may also be used for introducing new ideas, when planning, and for sharing learning outcomes (Berger, 1991).

3. Students are active learners and explorers, with teachers serving as guides in the exploration. Teachers work more as guides or facilitators of learning than as dispensers of information.

Tomlinson (1995, 1999) also noted that modifications of the general education can be made by offering students a range of learning tasks developed along one or more of the following continuums:

1. *Concrete to abstract tasks.* Gifted students frequently benefit from tasks that involve more abstract materials, representations, ideas, or applications than other students.

2. *Simple to complex tasks.* Gifted students tend to benefit from assignments that are more complex in resources, research, issues, problems, skills, or goals.

3. *Basic to transformational tasks.* Gifted students often learn more from tasks that require greater transformation or manipulation of information, ideas, materials, or applications than other students.

4. *Single-faceted to multifaceted tasks.* Gifted students appreciate tasks or assignments that have more steps or parts in their directions, connections within or across subjects, or planning and execution.

5. *Smaller mental leaps to larger leaps.* Gifted students tend to appreciate tasks that require greater mental leaps in application, insight, or transfer.

6. *More structured to less structured.* Gifted students learn more from assignments or tasks that are more open relative to procedures, solutions, decisions, and materials.

7. *Dependence to independence.* Gifted students learn when there is independence in planning, designing, and self-monitoring.

8. *Slower to faster pace.* Gifted students tend to benefit from acceleration, namely quick movement through prescribed materials and tasks. Hence compacting, telescoping, and grade or subject skipping may be used.

In the section just presented, we focused on strategies commonly recommended for effectively teaching gifted students. At the heart of these practices is the concept and practice of 'differentiation' supported by the belief that the needs of gifted students are sufficiently different from other students to warrant gifted education services. We turn, now, to the education of culturally diverse students.

Multicultural Education: Recommended Strategies for Teaching Culturally Diverse Students

The field of multicultural education, as a formal discipline, is rather new. It is a field of study and an emerging discipline whose major goal is to create educational opportunities for students from diverse racial, ethnic, social-class, and cultural groups (Banks, 1999; Banks & Banks, 1995).

One of the important goals of multicultural education is to help *all* students—not just culturally diverse students—to acquire the knowledge, attitudes, and skills needed to function effectively in a pluralistic democratic society and to interact, negotiate, and communicate with people from diverse groups. Ultimately, multicultural education seeks to create a civic and moral community that works for the common good (Banks & Banks, 1995, p. xi). These goals are consistent with our democratic principles of equity and justice. In essence, multicultural education seeks to put the words of these documents into reality.

Listening to Students: Why Education Must Be Multicultural

The most important and most effective way to determine the need for multicultural education is to listen to students. The results of two studies that examined the nature and extent of underachievement among gifted Black students have been published (Ford, 1993; Ford, 1995). Part of this examination included interviews with students regarding their perceptions of school curricula. The first study, conducted in one Ohio school district, consisted of fourth through sixth graders. The second study, conducted in five Virginia school districts, consisted of sixth through ninth graders.

When students in both studies offered comments on the curriculum, they were most likely to provide negative viewpoints. In both studies, the students' comments reflect common themes worth noting. First, most students noted a lack of mirrors for culturally diverse groups in the curriculum; that is, most of their education focus on the successes, contributions, accomplishments, and histories of White Americans. Students also noted that multicultural education, when addressed, was at the lowest levels of Banks' (1993) model—contributions and additive approaches (see Table 2). Students observed that their classes seldom emphasized minority groups other than African Americans. The Black students in both studies contend that classes consistently stressed the same minority heroes (e.g., Harriet Tubman, Martin Luther King, Jr.), while ignoring contemporary minority role models (e.g., Colin Powell, Barbara Clark, Nelson Mandela, Jesse Jackson) and controversial minority persons (e.g., Malcolm X, W.E.B. DuBois) and events (e.g., slave revolts). Students recognized that the superficial learning experiences also occurred primarily during February or Black History Month. Similarly, students distinguished the focus on historical events at the expense of pressing contemporary events. These narrow discussions do not help students to relate the past to the present or the future. The students noted that school is more interesting, engaging, motivating, and relevant when they learn about their own culture and the culture of others. In essence, students' comments tell us that they *want* more and they *need* more multicultural education. Their overarching questions were: Why am I learning this? How does this relate to me? How will this information help me now and in the future?

Students' comments provide important insights into what must be done to change curriculum and instruction. The students are telling us that they want their education to be relevant, meaningful, personal, and empowering. Students do not want to dwell on the past at the expense of the present and future. Ultimately, they want multiculturalism integrated throughout the curriculum in substantive ways and on a consistent basis. As one student questioned, "Is this too much to ask?" (Ford, 1996).

Questions to Consider Regarding Curriculum and Instruction

As Davidman and Davidman (1996) noted, teachers must ask at least four questions when assessing curriculum and instruction (i.e., lessons, materials, and strategies) for biases. These questions help guide changes in curriculum and instruction.

1. Do materials, lessons, and strategies promote educational equity? For instance, does the lesson help to create a curriculum where all students participate and contribute in substantive ways?

2. Do curriculum and instruction promote cultural pluralism or intergroup harmony in the classroom? Are students treated as equal members of the classroom community? Are cooperative strategies and groupings used to teach lessons and to promote positive, affirming student relationships?

3. Do curriculum and instruction help to increase students' knowledge regarding various cultural groups, including their own? Are mirrors (focus on self and own cultural group) and windows (focus on others and other cultural groups) provided so that learning is relevant, motivating, engaging, interesting, and empowering? And so that different perspectives are seen and heard?

4. Do curriculum and instruction help to correct distortions about minority groups? For example, are distortions discussed?

When designing the most appropriate educational experiences for culturally diverse students, at least three areas must be considered and then addressed: multicultural curricula considerations; multicultural instructional considerations; and culturally responsive learning environments. Before presenting these components, it must be noted that the notion of "differentiation" often discussed in gifted education applies equally as well to culturally diverse students. When addressing their specific educational needs, modifications to content, process, and learning environments must be made, as reflected in Table 1.

Multicultural Curriculum—Modifying Content

In general, a culturally responsive curriculum is one in which the materials, content, and resources used to teach students have a multicultural focus. As with differentiating the basic curriculum for gifted students, described earlier, multicultural education is also concerned with differentiation. Changes are made to the content of the curriculum, adding culturally diverse people, resources, books, events, topics, and issues.

The overall goal of a multicultural curriculum is to affirm students' identity, to increase their engagement, interest, and motivation in learning with the ultimate outcome being increased achievement. Few models exist that specifically

Table 1
Differentiating Content, Process, and Learning Environments in Gifted and Multicultural Education

	Gifted Education	Multicultural Education
Content	Content modified through the use of more advanced or complex concepts, abstractions, and materials.	Content modified to include greater focus on multicultural concepts, issues, themes, events, and people. Curricular resources and materials are multicultural.
Process	Activities are redesigned or restructured to be more intellectually demanding. High-level thinking, problem solving, inquiry-based learning are used, as well as acceleration.	Instructional strategies, including teaching styles, are modified to match more closely the learning and cognitive styles of culturally diverse students. Students' cultural backgrounds and characteristics are given substantive consideration in instructional practices.
Product	Students share their learning in varied ways, particularly by producing products that are authentic, address real issues, and have real audiences.	Students share their learning in many ways, but a multicultural focus is always present to some degree. Students develop products that address issues and solve problems germane to culturally diverse populations.
Learning Environment	Teachers create environments that are safe, nonjudgmental, and student-centered such that students are at ease in taking intellectual and creative risks. Teachers create a sense of community in which all gifts and talents are valued and respected.	Teachers create learning environments that affirm students' identity as cultural beings; teachers use the cultural characteristics of diverse groups to create a learning community where are individuals are valued and respected.

address ways to modify curriculum (Ford & Harris, 1999). However, Banks (1999) does offer a model that addresses multicultural curriculum modification (see Table 2).

Banks (1999) discussed four levels of integration of multicultural content into the curriculum. In the first level, the *Contributions Approach*, educators focus on heroes, holidays, and discrete elements. This is the most extensively used approach to multiculturalism in the schools. A central characteristic of this approach is that the traditional ethnocentric curriculum remains unchanged in its basic structure, goals, and salient characteristics. Students are introduced to culturally diverse heroes, such as Caesar Chavez; Martin Luther King, Jr.; and Booker T. Washington. Furthermore, individuals who challenged the predominant cultures' ideologies, values, and conceptions, and who advocated radical social, political, and economic reform are often ignored in this approach. As a result, Martin Luther King, Jr. is more likely to be discussed than Malcolm X; and Booker T. Washington is more likely to be discussed than W.E.B. DuBois. Subsequently, students acquire a distorted or incomplete view of history and reality.

Another characteristic of this low-level approach is that cultural traditions, foods, music, and dance may be discussed, but little or no attention is given to their meaning and significance to these culturally diverse groups. Also, ethnic content is limited primarily to special days, weeks, and months related to culturally diverse groups. Students learn nothing of substance about the occasion, group, or individuals being celebrated. The contributions approach is cosmetic; it provides teachers with a quick, nonthreatening way to integrate the curriculum, and teachers themselves can adopt this approach without knowing much about racially and culturally diverse groups. This approach also reinforces stereotypes about culturally diverse groups, while using safe, nonthreatening heroes found acceptable to those in positions of authority and power.

In the second level, the *Additive Approach*, the content, concepts, themes, and perspectives of culturally diverse groups are

Table 2
Approaches to Integrating Multicultural Content

Approach	Description	Examples
Contributions	Heroes, cultural components, holidays, and other discrete elements related to ethnic groups are added to the curriculum on special days, occasions, and celebrations.	• Famous minorities are studied only during certain times. • Little attention is devoted to the cultures in which the artifacts are embedded.
Additive	Consists of additions to the content, concepts, themes, and perspectives to the curriculum without changing its structure.	• Adding books and materials without reconceptualizing the unit or giving the students the background knowledge to understand the books or materials. • Adding a unit on an ethnic group without focusing on the group in other units. Leaving the core curriculum intact but adding an ethnic studies course, as an elective.
Transformation	The basic goals, structure, and nature of the curriculum are changed to enable students to view concepts, events, issues, problems, and themes from the perspectives of diverse groups.	• Units describe the meaning of events, issues, etc., to all groups involved. All voices are heard.
Social Action	Students identify important social problems and issues, gather pertinent data, clarify their values on the issues, make decisions, and take reflective actions to help resolve the issues or problem.	• Students study prejudice and discrimination in their school and take action to improve race relations. • Students study the treatment of culturally diverse groups and take action to redress inequities.

Note. From *Introduction to Multicultural Education* (2nd ed., p. 81), by J. A. Banks, 1999, Boston: Allyn and Bacon. Copyright ©1999 by Allyn and Bacon.

Strengths	Problems
• Provides a quick and easy way to put ethnic content into the curriculum. • Gives ethnic heroes visibility in the curriculum, alongside mainstream heroes. • Most frequently adopted in schools.	• Results in a superficial understanding of ethnic cultures. • Focuses on the lifestyles and artifacts of ethnic groups; reinforces stereotypes and misperceptions. • Mainstream criteria used to select heroes and cultural elements for inclusion in the curriculum.
• Makes it possible to add ethnic content into the curriculum without changing its structure. Requires substantial changes and staff development. • Can be implemented within the existing curriculum.	• Reinforces the idea that ethnic history and culture are not integral parts of the U.S. mainstream culture. • Students view ethnic groups from a Eurocentric perspective. • Fails to help students understand how the dominant culture and ethnic cultures are interconnected and inter-related.
• Enables students to understand the complex ways in which diverse groups participated in the formation of the U.S. society and culture. • Helps reduce racial and ethnic encapsulation. • Enables diverse groups to see their cultures, ethos, and perspectives in the school curriculum. • Gives students a balanced view of he nature and development of U.S. culture and society. • Helps to empower culturally diverse groups.	• Requires substantial curriculum revision, in-service training, and the identification and development of materials written from the perspectives of diverse groups. • Staff development for the institutionalization of this approach must be ongoing and continual.
• Enables students to improve their thinking, value analysis, decision-making skills, and social-action skills. • Enables students to improve their data gathering, social-actions, and problem-solving skills. • Helps students to develop a sense of political efficacy. • Helps students to improve their skills in working with diverse groups.	• Requires a considerable amount of curriculum planning and materials. • Longer in duration than more traditional teaching units. • May focus on problems and issues considered controversial. • Students may be unable to take meaningful actions that contribute to the resolution of some social issues and problems.

added to the curriculum without changing its structure. For instance, teachers may add a book, unit, or course to the curriculum that focuses on diverse groups or topics. While the content changes slightly, there is little restructuring of the curriculum relative to purposes and characteristics. Culturally diverse students learn little of their own history, and White students learn little of the history and contributions of other racial and cultural groups to American society. For instance, students reading *White Socks Only, Maizon at Blue Hill, The Autobiography of Malcolm X, Goin' Someplace Special, The Bluest Eyes, The Invisible Man, I Know Why the Caged Bird Sings, The Color Purple, To Kill a Mockingbird*, or *Native Son*, lack the concepts, content background, and emotional maturity to understand, appreciate, respect, and cope effectively with the concepts and issues discussed in the literature. The additive approach fails to help students view society from diverse perspectives and to understand the ways that the histories of the nation's diverse racial, cultural, ethnic, and religious groups are interconnected (Banks & Banks, 1995). This superficial approach requires little time, effort, training, or rethinking of curriculum and instruction.

In the third level, the *Transformational Approach*, the structure of the curriculum is changed to enable students to view concepts, issues, events, and themes from the perspectives of culturally diverse groups. This is a fundamental, substantive change from the previous two levels; one now sees changes in the basic assumptions, goals, nature, and structure of the curriculum. The fundamental goal of the transformation approach is to help all students to feel informed and empowered. According to Banks and Banks (1995), the curriculum must focus on how the common American culture and society emerged from a complex synthesis and interaction of the diverse cultural elements that make up the United States. This approach requires extensive curriculum revision, changes in teacher preparation, not to mention much time, effort, and commitment.

In the fourth level, the *Social Action Approach*, the focus is on taking action and addressing social injustices. Here, students make decisions on important social issues and take action to help solve them. Students are not socialized to accept mainstream ideologies, practices, and institutions. Instead, students–regardless of their age–feel empowered and are proactive; they are provided with the knowledge, values, resources, and skills necessary to participate in social change. Student self-examination becomes central in this approach through value analysis, decision-making, problem solving, and social action skills. For example, students examine issues surrounding prejudice and discrimination in order to develop ways to improve race relations. This approach is least likely to be adopted by educators, primarily because teachers lack formal training, experience, understanding, and personal knowledge of other racial and cultural groups (e.g., histories, values, beliefs, customs; Ford & Harris, 1999).

At the highest levels, the models described by Banks (1999) and Banks and Banks (1995) require extensive philosophical and curricular changes. Clearly, the most important reasons for multicultural education are its benefits to students. Multicultural education helps all students to accept their culture as an essential component of their personal development. While increasing their knowledge about cultural and racial diversity, students acquire an ethic of social justice–their sense of personal independence, social interdependence, personal responsibility, and social responsibility–that serves to increase their interest, motivation, and learning.

Multicultural Instruction—Modifying Process

Boykin (1994), Hale (2001), Shade, Kelly, and Oberg (1997), Ladson-Billings (1994), Milner (2003) and others have presented convincing research supporting the notion that culture influences learning styles and thinking styles. In his Afrocentric model, Boykin identified nine cultural styles commonly found among African Americans: spirituality, harmony, oral tradition, affective, communalism, verve, movement, social time perspective, and expressive individualism (see Table 3). Movement refers to African Americans being tactile and kinesthetic students who show a preference for being physically involved in learning experiences. They are active students who are engaged when they are physically and psychological involved; otherwise, they may be easily distracted and off task. Harmony refers to an ability to read the environment well, to read nonverbal behaviors proficiently. Thus, students who feel unwelcome in their classes may become unmotivated and disinterested in learning. Communalism refers to a social, extraverted, cooperative, interdependent style of living and learning such that competition (especially with friends) is devalued. Therefore, students with this learning preference may be unmotivated in highly individualistic and competitive classrooms, preferring to learn in groups rather than in isolation.

Accordingly, teachers should learn to modify their teaching styles to accommodate different learning styles. For example, to accommodate students' preference for communalism, teachers can use cooperative learning strategies and place students in groups when working on assignments; they might also need to decrease competition between students and encourage social or cooperative learning. To accommodate oral tradition, verve, and movement, teachers can give students opportunities to write and perform skits, conduct oral presentations, and participate in debates. Table 4 contains more specific instructional strategies.

Culturally Responsive Learning Environments—Modifying Environment

A culturally responsive learning environment is inclusive of multicultural curriculum and instruction. When these needs are addressed in a positive and proactive manner, the environment will be more respectful of and value student differences along cultural lines. Teachers whose learning environments are

Table 3
Boykin's Afrocentric Cultural Characteristics

Cultural Characteristic	Description
Spirituality	Belief in a nonmaterial force that influences all of life; religious; faithful; optimistic; resilient.
Harmony	Keen observation skills as demonstrated by: (1) ability to read the environment well and (2) ability to read people well (reads nonverbal cues and body language well); quickly notices injustices and discrepancies in what is said and done, as well as how students are treated.
Affective	Sensitive and emotional; easily excited; impulsive–may react before thinking. Easily angered; loves and hates strongly.
Movement	Enjoys being mobile and active; tactile and kinesthetic learners; dislikes being sedentary; prefers to be physically and mentally engaged.
Verve	High levels of energy; easily excited; physically active when engaged and mentally stimulated; can become "loud" when excited or engaged.
Communalism	A strong need to belong; strong need for affiliation; group oriented; social and interdependent; extraverted—people oriented. Want to be liked, appreciated, and respected by others. Sense of family and community is strong.
Expressive Individualism	Creative; risk taker; dares to be different; dramatic; clever; original. Likes to play with ideas, words, language, dressing, and to embellish what appears commonplace or bland.
Oral Tradition	Prefers to communicate orally; blunt with comments and feedback; direct with words and feedback or comments; likes playing with words (jokes, puns, riddles, proverbs, analogies, etc.).
Social Time Perspective	Polychronic; time is not seen as a limited commodity—there is unlimited time; time is social; time should be enjoyed; can do more than one thing at a time; may have difficulty with managing time and organization; pleasure and work go hand-in-hand.

Table 4
Multicultural and Culturally Responsive Instructional Strategies

Boykin's Afrocentric Characteristics	Teaching Strategies and Products
Movement Verve	• Creative movement (mime, drama, dance, tableau techniques–body used to communicate) • Hands-on thinking; manipulatives (e.g., sculpting) • Role-plays, simulations, drama/theatre • Field trips • Physical activity • Sports and games • Learning centers
Harmony Verve Expressive Individualism	• Singing, humming, whistling, chanting, tapping • Curriculum songs (creating melodies, songs, rap, cheers, jingles) • Background music • Playing instruments • Poetry/poems • Drama • Environmental and social issues • Graphic-rich environment (visuals and graphic organizers, pictures, posters, charts, graphs, diagrams) • Mind mapping (webbing) • Puzzles and games (e.g., Chess) • Painting, collages, visual arts
Social Time Perspective (polychronic)	• Structure—specificity and clarity; clear expectations and requirements • Authoritative and authoritarian teaching styles • Time-management and organization skills • Meaningful assignments, interest-based assignments • Choice • Humor, jokes • Deadlines with some flexibility • Assignments broken into steps with reminders of deadlines
Communalism Affective	• Social, peer, cooperative learning (e.g., clubs) • Competition with group/sports philosophy • Opportunity to help others (e.g., tutoring, mentoring) • Service and community involvement • Conflict resolution and mediation skills
Oral Tradition	• Discussions/Dialogues • Oral presentations and speeches; speakers • Debates • Socratic questioning • Scientific investigations and experiments • Logical-sequential assignments (reports, experiments, research) • Logical puzzles and games • Competitions with group philosophy • Analogies • Independent study projects • Word games (e.g., idioms, jokes, puns, riddles, homonyms, anagrams, mnemonics) • Poetry • Storytelling • Drama • Journal writing

culturally responsive are quite attentive to the cultural needs of their students (Gay & Kirkland, 2003). They develop policies and rules that promote appreciation of differences so that all students, particularly culturally diverse students, feel safe, valued, and respected. At the very least, when a classroom is culturally responsive, the following components are present:

1. Biased, stereotypical, or insensitive materials and language are avoided, or questioned if used.

2. Assessment or evaluation materials/tools are examined for potential biases and avoided if found.

3. All subject areas are infused with multicultural content and topics.

4. Teachers adapt their teaching styles to students' learning and/or cognitive styles; students are not penalized for differences in learning or cognitive styles.

5. Teachers do not let student differences interfere with teaching and learning; they try to consider these differences in planning lessons and activities, and in choosing topics and projects.

6. Teachers believe that students' self-concept, self-esteem, and racial identities are important to the learning process and try to create an identity-affirming climate.

7. Multiple perspectives are discussed on issues and events; no one point of view dominates.

8. Literature includes multicultural titles.

9. Materials are multicultural (e.g., flesh-colored crayons, paper, band-aids, etc.).

10. Culturally diverse persons or groups are consistently discussed in all subject areas.

11. Disrespect of fellow students is not tolerated and is followed up with consequences.

12. Students feel comfortable discussing issues of diversity.

13. A sense of family, community, and interdependence is present.

14. Teachers are comfortable working with students who are culturally diverse.

Multicultural Gifted Education: One Model

In Table 5, we present a model that combines aspects of gifted education and multicultural education using the work of Bloom (1956) and Banks (1999). By combining the levels of both Bloom's Taxonomy and Banks, Ford and Harris (1999) created a matrix from which educators can begin to develop curriculum that impacts students cognitively (Bloom's levels) and multiculturally (Banks' framework). Ford and Harris maintain that curriculum based on this model can fall into four categories: (1) low levels in both challenge and diversity or multiculturalism; (2) low level in challenge but high level in multiculturalism; (3) low level in multiculturalism but high level in challenge; and (4) high levels for both diversity and challenge. For example, a lesson plan that has high levels of challenge might focus on analysis, synthesis, and evaluation, but only when it comes to music or artifacts from a cultural group (e.g., compare and contrast the Black National Anthem with the National Anthem of the United States). A lesson plan that asks students to observe or research how Hispanic males are treated in a mall and then to speak with store owners would be high level on Bloom's Taxonomy (evaluation) and high level in multiculturalism because students share their concerns in order to seek changes (Banks' social action level). A lesson that simply asks students to identify dates and events in the Civil Rights Movement is potentially low level on both accounts (see Ford & Harris, 1999, for more specific examples, including sample lesson plans using the matrix).

Table 5
Ford-Harris Matrix Using Bloom-Banks Model:
Definition/Description of Categories

	Knowledge	Comprehension	Application	Analysis	Synthesis	Evaluation
Contributions	Students are taught and know facts about cultural artifacts, events, groups, and other cultural elements.	Students show an understanding of information about cultural artifacts, groups, etc.	Students are asked to and can apply information learned on cultural artifacts, events, etc.	Students are taught to and can analyze (e.g., compare and contrast) information about cultural artifacts, groups, etc.	Students are required to and can create a new product from the information on cultural artifacts, groups, etc.	Students are taught to and can evaluate facts and information based on cultural artifacts, groups, etc.
Additive	Students are taught and know concepts and themes about cultural groups.	Students are taught and can understand cultural concepts and themes.	Students are required to and can apply information learned about cultural concepts and themes.	Students are taught to and can analyze important cultural concepts and themes.	Students are asked to and can synthesis important information on cultural concepts and themes.	Students are taught to and can critique cultural concepts and themes.
Transformation	Students are given information on important cultural elements, groups, etc., and can understand this information from different perspectives.	Students are taught to understand and can demonstrate an understanding of important cultural concepts and themes from different perspectives.	Students are asked to and can apply their understanding of important concepts and themes from different perspectives.	Students are taught to and can examine important cultural concepts and themes from more than one perspective.	Students are required to and can create a product based on their new perspective or the perspective of another group.	Students are taught to and can evaluate or judge important cultural concepts and themes from different viewpoints (e.g., minority group).
Social Action	Based on information on cultural artifacts, etc., students make recommendations for social action.	Based on their understanding of important concepts and themes, students make recommendations for social action.	Students are asked to apply their understanding of important social and cultural issues; they make recommendations for and take action on these issues.	Students are required to and can analyze social and cultural issues from different perspectives; they take action on these issues.	Students create a plan of action to address a social and cultural issue(s); they seek important social change.	Students critique important social and cultural issues, and seek to make national and/or international change.

Note. From *Multicultural Gifted Education* (p. 80), by D. Y. Ford & J. J. Harris III, 1999, New York: Teachers College Press. Copyright ©1999 Teachers College Press.

Actions taken on the social action level can range from immediate and small scale (e.g., classroom and school level) to moderate (e.g., community or regional level) to large scale (state, national, and international levels). Likewise, students can make recommendations for action or actually take social action

Profiles of Multicultural Teachers

All teachers can be effective, competent multicultural educators. Many educators, representing all cultural backgrounds, have been noted for their work in promoting equity and excellence in teaching students of color. Like Davidman and Davidman (1994) and Ford and Harris (1999), we are particularly interested in the works of Marva Collins, Philip Uri Treisman, James P. Comer, and Jaime Escalante, all of whom demonstrated that excellence and equity can co-exist in harmony, and that high expectations are powerful components of multicultural teaching.

Marva Collins

Marva Collins is known for her phenomenal and exceptional teaching of Black children for more than 30 years. She is a pioneer in education—a true educator, teacher, and mentor—who emphasizes high expectations, strong self-concept, and firm discipline. Employing a hands-on approach to teaching, she is the founder and director of the Westside Preparatory

School in Chicago, Illinois that was founded in 1975. She began her teaching career in Alabama, teaching for two years, and then moved to Chicago where she taught in the public school system for 14 years.

What is so remarkable is that Marva Collins educated the children who may have been labeled "unreachable and unteachable" by many in a public school context. For instance, according to an article in *Ebony* magazine, Collins took "in learning disabled, problem children and even one child labeled border-line retarded. At the end of the first year, every child scored at least five grades higher proving that the previous labels placed on these children were misguided" (Kinnon, 1996, p. 122). Her hard work, dedication, and no-nonsense philosophies and teaching approaches seemed to work and to counter negative predictions about where her students would eventually end up in adulthood. For instance, statistically, her first 33 students should have been in jail, dead, or on welfare. However, *all* 33 of these students excelled and are doing quite well in their respective lives and careers. Marva Collins is, indeed, the ultimate and true educator.

Philip Uri Treisman

Treisman, a professor at the University of Texas, Austin, and a former math educator, dramatically improved the academic achievement of Black students after analyzing and studying the differential math achievement of two different racial groups. In 1975, while working with teaching assistants at the University of California at Berkeley, Treisman found that 60% of the Black students were failing freshman calculus compared to 12% for Chinese students. His search for an explanation of this large discrepancy led to a doctoral dissertation in which he observed and videotaped 20 Black and 20 Chinese students in their dorms and other settings as they worked on math assignments.

After 18 months of observation and interviewing, Treisman discovered that the major difference in their pattern of success was the way students interacted with each other when studying. The majority of the Black students (18 out of 20) never studied with other students and attributed their success to studying in isolation, that is, separating studying from socialization. Conversely, 13 out of 20 Chinese students adopted support-oriented study patterns that included socialization.

Based on these findings, Treisman developed and refined an equity workshop strategy that allowed students to study math under the guidance of a skilled teacher and within a community of peers. Results indicated that the 60% failure rate of culturally diverse students dropped to 4%, and that, over the last decade, the culturally diverse students in the workshops have performed better than other students. Thirty colleges and universities have adopted the workshop in such courses as physics, chemistry, engineering, and math.

Treisman personifies multicultural teaching by not accepting the failure rates of culturally diverse students and by taking active steps to reverse those rates. By not accepting the students' failure and by seeking to understand the outcomes, Treisman attributed poor outcomes to external rather than internal factors.

James P. Comer

In the late 1960s, Dr. Comer noted that two Black elementary schools ranked near the bottom in terms of achievement and attendance out of 33 New Haven elementary schools. Further, teacher attrition was among the highest in the state, with 25% leaving per year, and parents were described as dejected, angry, distrustful, and alienated. Within 7 years, Comer and his colleagues at Yale University developed a prevention and intervention plan, which included mental health professionals, parents, administrators, and teachers. Like Treisman, Comer did not adopt a deficit orientation to his thinking about and work with students. He did not blame children for their failures; he did not perceive the major problem as low achievement, low attendance, and low morale. Instead, these variables were perceived as symptoms of a greater underlying problem. Comer's team diagnosed the major problem as the schools' failure to pay attention to the psychological development of students, and the lack of positive relationships between the school and home (i.e., cultural discontinuity or mismatch). Having connected the problems with the symptoms, Dr. Comer developed a governance and management team that included all stakeholders in the decisions affecting students; hence, all partners had a sense of ownership in the school and its operations. By 1979, the students who had ranked the lowest in achievement among the 33 schools had reached their grade level by the fourth grade. By 1984, students in the fourth grade ranked third and fourth highest on the Iowa Test of Basic Skills.

Functioning from a multicultural perspective, Comer noted that race, culture, socioeconomic status, and self-esteem were powerful variables in the learning process. Equally important, he recognized that sociocultural forces, including a mismatch between the home and school, could wreak havoc on culturally diverse students' achievement. This cultural discontinuity resulted in student failures and conflicts. Comer was able to see the cultural nature of the problem from a proactive view rather than adopting a cultural deficit perspective.

Jaime Escalante

Escalante was a mathematics teacher. When he began teaching in Los Angeles, Escalante worked with a predominantly Latino student body. Approximately three fourths of the students were eligible for free or reduced lunch. Most students failed to pass the AP Calculus exam in 1977. One year later, four in seven students passed. By 1989, 66% passed. No comparable high school in the nation performed as well.

In raising test scores and operating from a multicultural perspective, Escalante addressed the goals of educational equity and the creation of collaborative, empowering relationships among parents, teachers, and students. Escalante sought to demonstrate that Mexican American students whose parents had low educational levels could perform as well as middle-class, highly educated students. Escalante also adopted the role of mentor and role model. Escalante was available prior to school, during lunch hours, and after school; he provided educational services, with parental permission, to students up to three hours after school ended, without additional pay. For Escalante, student achievement was the reward. The primary message communicated to students was high expectations and self-affirmation.

Summary and Conclusion

There is a wealth of talent and intelligence in this field
[of gifted education], but I worry that we are using it to
defend yesterday, not to imagine and build tomorrow.

—Borland (1996, p. 145)

The pedagogical clock for all students is running. As advocates of students with exceptional and diverse needs, we must more actively and more proactively address the unique and special needs of our students. To do so requires a broadened and comprehensive notion of gifted students. Stated another way, a colorblind or culture-blind philosophy, has failed to identify and serve students who are gifted *and* culturally diverse (Ford et al., 2003). African American, Hispanic American, Native American and Asian American gifted students have cognitive, affective, and instructional needs like White gifted students, but they also have different needs. To ignore, negate, or minimize these differences is to ignore these students. In essence, our field exists because of student differences; the rationale for the field of gifted education has been the need to address the various needs of students who are different. *If gifted students were like all other students, there would be no need for gifted education.* And just as we are willing to address gender and economic differences to better identify and serve gifted students, we must be willing–no less eager–to acknowledge and address cultural differences.

In the previous pages, we built upon bodies of work on gifted students by describing promising practices for working with students who are not only gifted, but also culturally diverse. Gifted students are gifted 24 hours a day, seven days of the week. Likewise, culturally diverse students are culturally diverse 24 hours a day, seven days of the week. Thus, we maintain that the most effective way to teach and reach these students is to consider the combined needs associated with being gifted on the one hand and being diverse on the other. The strategies described borrowed from two fields of education: gifted education and urban or multicultural education. In effect, we have bridged two fields to meet the dual needs of our culturally diverse gifted students. The pedagogical clock is ticking for all students. Let us use our time—and our students' time—wisely. A mind is terrible thing to waste; a mind is a terrible thing to erase (Ford & Harris, 1999).

Web Sites

Anti-Defamation League
http://www.adl.org

Combats anti-Semitism and bigotry of all kinds.

Joint Center for Poverty Research
http://www.jcpr.org

Supports academic research that examines what it means to be poor and live in America.

National Association for Multicultural Education
http://www.nameorg.org

Brings together individuals and groups with an interest in multicultural education from all levels of education, different academic disciplines and from diverse educational institutions and occupations.

North Central Regional Educational Laboratory
http://www.ncrel.org

A nonprofit organization dedicated to helping schools, and the students they serve, reach their full potential.

Teaching Tolerance
http://www.tolerance.org

Promotes and supports antibias activism in every venue of American life.

Publications

Journal of Negro Education
http://www.journalnegroed.org

A scholarly journal on issues and concerns related to the education of African American people in the United States and in developing countries.

Multiple Voices for Ethnically Diverse Exceptional Learners
http://www.cec.sped.org/dv/ddel.html

A biannual publication of interest to special education professionals serving culturally and linguistically diverse learners with disabilities and/or who have gifts and talents.

African Americans' Struggle for Equality [series]
(Anna Wilson, 1992, grades 6–12)

This series describes the African American experience and

the ongoing struggle for equality in education, employment, politics, and the criminal justice system.

Videos About Social Issues

Behind the Mask
(8 minutes, Anti-Defamation League, 1986, grades 5–6)

Helps students understand the concepts of prejudice and stereotyping.

Beyond Hate and *The Heart of Hatred*
(52 minutes, Films for the Humanities & Sciences, with Bill Moyer, 2003, grades 7–12)

These two videos help students explore the origins and dimensions of hate, through the eyes of world leaders, human rights activities, students, gangs, and supremacist groups.

Breaking Through Stereotypes
(15 minutes, Edcucational Video Center, 1994, grades 7–12)

Produced by and for teens, this documentary explores how stereotypes influence human interaction.

Crimes of Hate,
(30 minutes, Anti-Defamation League, 1990, grades 7–12)

Explores hate groups, their motivation, and the devastating impact of their actions.

How We're Different and Alike
(10 minutes, United Learning, 1994, grades 1–6)

Features four children of diverse ethnic backgrounds

exploring the things they all have in common and those that make them different from each other.

Learning to Hate
(39 minutes, Anti-Defamation League, 1997, grades 7–12)

Is hatred taught? This video focuses on how children learn to hate, and how attitudes about hatred differ from culture to culture.

Many Voices: The World at My Door
(28 minutes, TVOntario, 1991, grades 4–6)

When her classmates make fun of her new haircut, a young girl learns that prejudice is an important issue in her life even though the town she lives in is ethnically homogeneous.

Personal Ethics and the Future of the World
(29 minutes, Kinetic Inc., 1991, grades 7–12)

Hosted by Meg Ryan, this video and guide explores the ways in which personal ethics and individual actions affect the rest of the world.

Prejudice: Answering Children's Questions
(75 minutes, MPI Home Video, 1992, grades 5–8)

This program, hosted by Peter Jennings, features a panel of students asking questions about prejudice. Also explores the experiences of students and their encounters with prejudice.

Quick to Judge
(15 minutes, Beacon Films, 1992, grades 5–6)

Illustrates the damaging power of prejudice through the

eyes of a young African American male who is wrongfully accused of stealing.

Skin
(29 minutes, Landmark Films, 1989, grades 7–12)

This award-winning video explores the difficulties encountered by teenagers who are easily identified by their skin color as members of a minority group.

Appendix I: White Socks Only
A Literature Unit for Grades 3–5

by Evelyn Coleman, Donna Y. Ford, and Edna F. Thomas

Overview of Lesson Plan

As the nation becomes increasingly diverse, students (all people) are being challenged and encouraged to live in a diverse world, a world that looks different from the time when our parents and grandparents were children.

This lesson encourages children to think about the past—our nation's history—so that the negative events are never repeated. Likewise, students have an opportunity to think about the future, about making the world a better place for us all. Burying or ignoring the past will not make it go away. The past is part of who we are and why we are. Remembering the past can make us stronger. *White Socks Only* tells the story of child, now a grandmother, as she relives an event in her past. This is an event that must not be repeated; it is an event from which we all can learn.

Objectives

Students will be introduced to multicultural children's literature. They will gain a better understanding of the condition of life prior to desegregation. They will gain a better appreciation for why segregation ended. They will see that children can also make a difference in the world.

Processes/Skills

- Basic thinking skills (knowledge, comprehension, application)
- Critical thinking skills (analysis, synthesis, evaluation)
- Multicultural awareness and understanding
- Concept-based
- Interdisciplinary

Summary of Book

A grandmother shares a true and significant event in her childhood with her granddaughter. The grandmother recalls facing discrimination in the South when she was not allowed to drink from a water fountain with a sign that read: "Whites Only." Misunderstanding the sign, the girl thinks it is referring to white socks only. The event results in the sign being removed, and changes the life of the town.

Prereading Activities

Discuss important terms and concepts with students.

- What is segregation? Desegregation? Give examples of each.

- What was life like for Blacks during segregation? What

about for Whites? What were Blacks not allowed to do before desegregation?

- When did segregation become unconstitutional, illegal?

- Talk to students about famous Blacks during this era: Rosa Parks; Ruby Bridges; Dr. Martin Luther King, Jr.; and others involved in the Civil Rights Movement. Many of these names will be familiar to students. Ask students to think about how the persons were similar. What were all of them seeking?

- Give students the "ABC Famous African Americans" (see Appendix II). (This list can be used for other assignments, such as biographies). Using the list, let students create a timeline.

- In small groups of 2 or 3 students, write a report and make a presentation on how one of the people on the ABC list made a contribution to society.

- Remind students that Ruby Bridges is one of few children who helped to end segregation. Inform students that they are going to read about another child who influenced desegregation.

- Let children know that the book is written in southern dialect. Share some of the words and phrases with students. Let students know that people speak differently in different parts of the country.

Vocabulary

Segregation	Porch	Plaits	Hobbled
Plopped	Slinking down	Strutting	Bandanna
Chime	Desegregation		

1. Place the words into categories based on parts of speech.

2. Use different tenses of the verbs in sentences.

3. Give the antonym and synonym for the words.

Social Studies (prereading)

1. Hold a discussion about the major events leading up to desegregation in 1954 (*Brown vs. Topeka Board of Education*). Place these events on a timeline. Let students look at the cover of the book and estimate when this story might have taken place. Plot this on the timeline. Putting the events in a time frame will help students to understand the attitudes and beliefs of that time/era.

2. The event/incident takes place in Mississippi. Where is Mississippi? Is this a northern or southern state? What is the state flower, bird, etc.? Who is the governor of Mississippi?

3. As children read, ask them to think about time. How long ago did this incident take place? About how many years/decades ago?

4. Inform students of different beliefs between the north and the south prior to desegregation. How did most southerners feel about Blacks prior to desegregation? How did many northerners feel about desegregation?

5. Talk to children about making generalizations. What is a generalization? Share an example of a syllogism with students so they can consider the consequences of 'if then' thinking. For example,

> *All dogs bark.*
> *Milo is a dog.*
> *Therefore, Milo barks.*

5. Hold discussions about the accuracy of this syllogism. Is the first premise true? Is the second premise true? Is the conclusion true? Let students create their own syllogisms or give them a list to evaluate.

6. Extend the concept of generalizations to slavery and the north and south. Did *all* people in the south want to keep slaves? Did *all* people in the north want to end slavery?

7. Do you think that children today can make a difference in improving society? How?

8. What have you done that is courageous and made a difference in someone's life?

9. Research a young person in your town who has done a great and courageous deed. Send him/her a letter commending his/her efforts.

Lesson: White Socks Only

1. Who is the main character? What was she going to do with the eggs?

2. What is the story about? Retell the events.

3. What did she think the sign "Whites only" meant? What did it really mean? Do these signs still exist today? Why not?

4. Who was the Chicken Man? Why was he important in

the story? When you first read about him, what did you think? Now that you've read the book, how has your perception/opinion of him changed?

5. What is the main idea or the moral of the story?

6. Capture the essence of the story by writing a newspaper headline.

7. Create a newspaper or TV interview about the incident. In small groups, have students develop interview questions for the little girl, her mother, Chicken Man, or another character.

8. What did Mama mean when she said, "Well, I guess you can go to town by yourself now 'cause you're old enough to do some good"?

9. Do you think the girl did "some good"? How did the girl's mistake/misunderstanding change the lives of people in her town?

10. The incident with the water fountain happened many years ago. How did the little girl's effort help you or affect your life today? Write a letter to the little girl. In the letter, express your appreciation.

11. What have you learned about segregation? Why is desegregation important in schools?

12. How can you/we "do some good" in our classroom? In our school? In our neighborhood?

13. Create a magic potion or solution that will cure the ills of prejudice and send it to the Governor and President to help with their race-relations programs.

14. What have you learned about yourself? Using a Venn Diagram, compare yourself to the young girl—how are you similar and how are you different?

15. What did you like about the book? What did you dislike? What would you change about the book? (e.g., Would you change the ending?)

Science

1. Can you really fry an egg on the sidewalk? How can we find out?

2. Create a magic potion to cure prejudice. What would be the ingredients?

Visual and Performing Arts

1. Have students reenact the incident. Let students role play the characters and/or use tableau techniques.

2. Have students analyze and discuss the pictures. How has the author captured the emotions of the event?

3. Which picture did they like the most and the least? Why?

4. Examine the monuments shown in the book. Do a study of these monuments. Why do we create monuments? What other monuments have you seen?

5. Using clay or paint, make a monument of the little girl (and/or Chicken Man). What will you call the monument? Why might the little girl deserve to have a monument in her honor?

Interliterary Link

Read *The Story of Ruby Bridges*.

1. How is the life of the child in *White Socks Only* similar to the life of Ruby Bridges? (Likewise, how is she similar to Rosa Parks?) Create a Venn diagram to show the similarities and differences. What characteristics and supports did each child have that enabled her to persevere? Do we still have those characteristics and abilities? How can we show this?

2. Have Ruby Bridges and the little girl meet on a TV show. What would they have to say to each other? Create interview questions for them. Who would be the interviewer (e.g., student, Martin Luther King, Jr.)?

Home Connection

*   Have students ask family members about their lives as children before 1954. What has changed since their parents were children?

*   Have children interview grandparents. Did they ever see signs that read "Whites only"? When? Where?

*   Ask parents to share memorabilia of that era.

Appendix II: ABC's of Famous African Americans

A   Louis Armstrong
     Maya Angelou
     Arthur Ashe
     Marian Anderson

B   Benjamin Banneker
     James Baldwin
     Senator Edward Brooks
     Mary Macleod Bethune

C   George Washington Carver

D   Frederick Douglass
     Charles Drew
     Paul Lawrence Dunbar

E   Duke Ellington
     Ralph Ellison
     Marian Wright Edelman

F   James Forten

G   Arthur Gaston
    Marcus Garvey

H   Lionel Hampton
    Zora Neale Hurston
    Langston Hughes

I   Isabella

J   James Weldon Johnson
    Jesse Jackson
    Barbara Jordan
    James Earl Jones

K   Dr. Martin Luther King, Jr.

L   Joe Louis

M   Garrett A. Morgan
    Nelson Mandela
    Thurgood Marshall

N   James Nabrit

O   Jesse Owens

P   Rosa Parks
    Colin Powell
    Leontyne Price

Q   Benjamin Quarles

R   Jackie Robinson
    Paul Robeson

S   Bessie Smith

T   Harriet Tubman
     Sojourner Truth
     Nat Turner

U   Father Charles Uncles

V   Gustavus Vassa

W   Phyllis Wheatley
     Douglas Wilder
     Madame C.J. Walker
     Richard Wright

X   Malcolm X

Y   Whitney Young
     Andrew Young

Z   Roosevelt Zanders

Note. From Ford and Harris (1999).

by J. Spinelli

Objectives

- Students will learn about true friendships.

- Students will understand the effects of prejudice on people's lives.

- Students will learn how to make a positive difference in society.

- Students will distinguish between myth and reality.

Key Concepts

- Prejudice
- Stereotypes
- Cross-cultural friendships
- Myth
- Empowerment
- Social responsibility

Vocabulary

- Have students generate a list of vocabulary words or prepare a list for them.

  Sample:

Kaboodle	Frayed	Befuddled
Gauntlet	Ambled	Emanations
Pandemonium	Wiseacre	Mirage
Languished	Stoic	Filigreed
Meandering	Pommel	Pungent
Trestle	Blarney	Shinnied
Beseeching	Nonchalantly	Infamous
Flaunting	Converged	Bickered
Repertoire	Poleax	Ludicrous
Marauding	Extort	Shenanigans
Blemish	Grouse	Cardinal
Lambasting	Chaotic	

- Give students the option of a) defining the words and using them in sentences; b) finding synonyms for the words, and using them in sentences; c) finding antonyms, if possible.

Questions for Discussion

Part I

1. Based on the book cover, what do you think the book is about?

2. What is a "maniac"? How does Magee fit this definition?

3. What does the phrase "legends are made, not born" mean?

4. How was Jeffrey's early life traumatic? How does he seem to handle the difficulties?

5. How did Jeffrey get the name "Maniac"? Do you think the name is befitting?

6. Describe the town. How is it divided and why? What does segregation mean? In what ways does the book talk about segregation? How does Magee seem to feel about the segregated town?

7. Why is the knot so important to Maniac?

8. Why does Maniac leave town after he unties Cobble's knot? Would you have left?

9. What is the significance of the knot?

10. Is Magee difficult to figure out? What makes him so complex?

11. Why does Mars have such a hard time understanding Magee?

12. Why does the rag picker tell Magee to go back to his "own kind"? What does this phrase (own kind) mean?

13. What is the main problem that people in the story have to overcome?

Social Studies

1. Remind students that the book is about a crusade in some ways. What is a crusade? What crusade might students consider launching in their neighborhood?

2. Have students locate Valley Forge, Pennsylvania on the map; locate other places mentioned (Hollidaysburg, Cinshohocken, Bridgeport, Schuykill River, etc.) and trace Magee's travels.

Part II

1. Why doesn't Magee want to go to school?

2. Why does he paint numbers on the door of the equipment room?

3. Why does Grayson scrape Magee's arms? Does this make sense to you? Was Grayson serious? What does this action tell you about stereotypes?

4. How does Magee bring meaning to Grayson's life? Why is Christmas so special for them?

5. Besides Cobble's knot, what other kind of knot is Magee trying to untie?

6. What characteristics do you see in Magee? Are these worthy characteristics? Do you dislike or admire them?

7. Do you see yourself in Magee in any way? What are your own personal characteristics?

Part III

1. How does Magee change the lives of Russell and Piper?

2. How could going to the east end cause trouble? Does going on the other side of town bother Magee? How do you know this? What support can you find in the book?

3. How does Mars become a hero to the McNab brothers?

4. How are people's assumptions about Finsterwald like those regarding race/ethnicity?

5. Why does Magee abandon the McNabs?

6. Interpret the following statement: "Now there was something else in that house, and it smelled worse than garbage and turds." To what was Magee referring?

7. How does Maniac's problem with the trestle make him more real to Mars?

8. How has Maniac changed from the first time he went to the east end?

9. Was Magee right to bring Mars to the McNabs' party? Would you have done this? Explain you response.

10. Why do Amanda and Magee become friends? Magee and Mars? Magee and the brothers?

11. What is Maniac Magee's legacy? How did he make a difference in that town?

12. Is it possible to decrease/eliminate racial prejudice? Do you think Magee's strategies were effective? Are they possible in real life?

13. Having read the book, do you think the title "Maniac Magee" is appropriate? Is he a maniac?

Extensions

1. Write an essay or poem on the topic "What makes a friend."

2. What other ways might Magee have brought the two parts of the town together? What can we do to build friendships and increase understanding among people from different racial groups or cultures?

3. What parts of the book seem real/fact versus unreal/legend? Make two columns "Maniac the Legend" and "Jeffrey Magee the Boy" (e.g., Maniac is born in Bridgeport; Maniac wins a race against Mars by running backwards; Maniac does not go to school; Maniac scores 49 touchdowns).

4. If you could write a different ending to the book, what would it be?

5. In small groups, have students create a table of contents for the book. Give them an opportunity to share their tables.

6. The book contains many metaphors (remind students that metaphors differ from similes). Have students create a list of the metaphors, along with interpretations (Cobble's knot; Amanda's torn page; Finsterwald's yard, etc.).

7. Have students create a crossword puzzle of key terms in the book. Some students may wish to focus on words related to Magee's character or some specific topic/concept.

Banks, J. A. (1999). An *introduction to multicultural education* (2nd ed.). Boston: Allyn and Bacon.

Banks, J. A., & Banks, C. A. M. (Eds.). (1995). *Handbook of research on multicultural education*. New York: Macmillan.

Berger, S. L. (1991). *Differentiating curriculum for gifted students*. ERIC Document ED342175 (ERIC Digest #E510). Reston, VA: Council for Exceptional Children.

Bloom, B. S. (Ed.). (1956). *Taxonomy of educational objectives: The classification of educational goals*. New York: Longman.

Borland, J. H. (1996). Gifted education and the threat of irrelevance. *Journal for the Education of the Gifted, 16,* 129–147.

Boykin, A. W. (1994). Afrocultural expression and its implications for schooling. In E. R. Hollins, J. E. King, & W. C. Hayman (Eds.), *Teaching diverse populations: Formulating a knowledge base* (pp. 225–273). Albany: State University of New York Press.

Colangelo, N., & Davis, G. A. (2003). *Handbook of gifted education*. Boston: Allyn and Bacon.

Davidman, L., & Davidman, P. T. (1994). *Teaching with a multi-cultural perspective: A practical guide.* New York: Longman.

Davis, G. A., & Rimm, S. B. (2004). *Education of the gifted and talented.* Boston: Pearson.

Ford, D. Y. (1996). *Reversing underachievement among gifted Black students: Promising practices and programs.* New York: Teachers College Press.

Ford, D. Y. (1998). The under-representation of minority students in gifted education: Problems and promises in recruitment and retention. *The Journal of Special Education, 32,* 4–14.

Ford, D. Y., Grantham, T. C., & Harris III, J. J. (1998). Multicultural gifted education: A wakeup call to the profession. *Roeper Review, 19,* 72–78.

Ford, D. Y. & Harris III, J. J. (1999). *Multicultural gifted education.* New York: Teachers College Press.

Ford, D. Y., Harris, J. J., III, Tyson, C. A., & Frazier Trotman, M. (2002). Beyond deficit thinking: Providing access for gifted African American students. *Roeper Review, 24,* 52–58.

Ford, D. Y., Howard, T. C., Harris III, J. J., & Tyson, C. A. (2000). Creating culturally responsive classrooms for gifted minority students. *Journal for the Education of the Gifted, 23*(4), 397–427.

Ford, D. Y. (2002). Creating culturally responsive classrooms for gifted students. *Our Gifted Children, 91,* 5–10.

Frasier, M. M., Garcia, J. H., & Passow, A. H. (1995). *A review of assessment issues in gifted education and their implications for identifying gifted minority students.* Storrs: The National Research Center on the Gifted and Talented, University of Connecticut.

Frasier, M. M. & Passow, A. H. (1994). *Toward a new paradigm for identifying talent potential.* Storrs: The National Research Center on the Gifted and Talented, University of Connecticut.

Gallagher, J. J. (1988). National agenda for educating gifted students: Statement of priorities. *Exceptional Children, 55,* 107–114.

Gay, G., & Kirkland, K. (2003). Developing cultural critical consciousness and self-reflection in preservice teacher education. *Theory Into Practice, 42*, 181–187.

Hale, J. E. (2001). *Learning while Black: Creating educational excellence for African American children.* Baltimore, MD: Johns Hopkins University Press.

Karnes, F. A., & Stephens, K. R. (1999). *The ultimate guide to student product development and evaluation.* Waco, TX: Prufrock Press.

Karnes, F. A., & Bean, S. M. (2004). *Process Skills Rating Scales: Revised.* Waco, TX: Prufrock Press.

Kinnon, J. B. (1996). Marva Collins: The Collins creed. (Teaching that works). *Ebony, 52*(2), 122–125.

Ladson-Billings, G. (1994). *Dreamkeepers: Successful teachers of African American children.* San Francisco: Jossey-Bass.

Maker, C. J., & Nielson, A. B. (1995). *Curriculum development and teaching strategies for gifted learners* (2nd ed.). Austin, TX: PRO-ED.

Milner, H. R. (2003). A case study of an African American English teacher's cultural comprehensive knowledge and (self) reflective planning. *Journal of Curriculum and Supervision, 18*, 175–196.

National Association for Gifted Children (NAGC). (1994). *Differentiation of curriculum and instruction.* Washington, DC: Author.

National Association for Gifted Children (NAGC). (1995). *Addressing affective needs of gifted children.* Washington, DC: Author.

National Commission on Excellence in Education. (1983). *A nation at risk: The imperative for educational reform.* Washington, DC: U.S. Department of Education.

Passow, A. H., & Frasier, M. M. (1996). Toward improving identification of talent potential among minority and disadvantaged students. *Roeper Review, 18*, 198–202.

Paul, R., & Elder, L. (2002). *Critical thinking: Tools for taking charge of your personal and professional life.* Upper Saddle River, NJ: Prentice Hall.

Shade, B. J., Kelly, C., & Oberg, M. (1997). *Creating culturally responsive classrooms.* Washington, DC: American Psychological Association.

Silverman, L. K. (Ed.). (1993). *Counseling the gifted and talented.* Denver, CO: Love.

Tomlinson, C. A. (1995). *How to differentiate instruction in mixed-ability classrooms.* Alexandria, VA: Association for Supervision and Curriculum Development.

Tomlinson, C. A. (1999). *The differentiated classroom: Responding to the needs of all learners.* Alexandria, VA: Association for Supervision and Curriculum Development.

Tomlinson, C. A., Ford, D. Y., Reis, S. M., Briggs, C. J., & Strickland, C. A. (Eds.). (2004). *In search of the dream: Designing schools and classrooms that work for high potential students from diverse cultural backgrounds.* Washington, DC: National Association for Gifted Children.

VanTassel-Baska, J. (1994). *Comprehensive curriculum for gifted learners* (2nd ed.). Boston: Allyn and Bacon.

Zirkel, P. A., & Stevens, P. L. (1987). The law concerning public education of gifted students. *Journal for the Education of the Gifted, 10,* 305–322.

Donna Y. Ford received her degrees from Cleveland State University, where she focused on urban education and gifted education. Donna is Betts Chair of Education and Human Development in the Peabody College of Education, Vanderbilt University. She has three books and numerous articles that are designed to increase the achievement of gifted minority students and improve their representation in gifted education. She focuses on identification and assessment, underachievement, equity issues, multicultural education, and family involvement. Dr. Ford consults with school districts nationally, serves on the board of numerous professional organizations, and has received several awards for her work.

H. Richard Milner earned his Ph.D. from The Ohio State University in Curriculum Studies. He is assistant professor in the Department of Teaching and Learning at Peabody College of Vanderbilt University. His research interests concern teachers' influences in students' opportunities to learn and academic achievement and persistence among African American students.